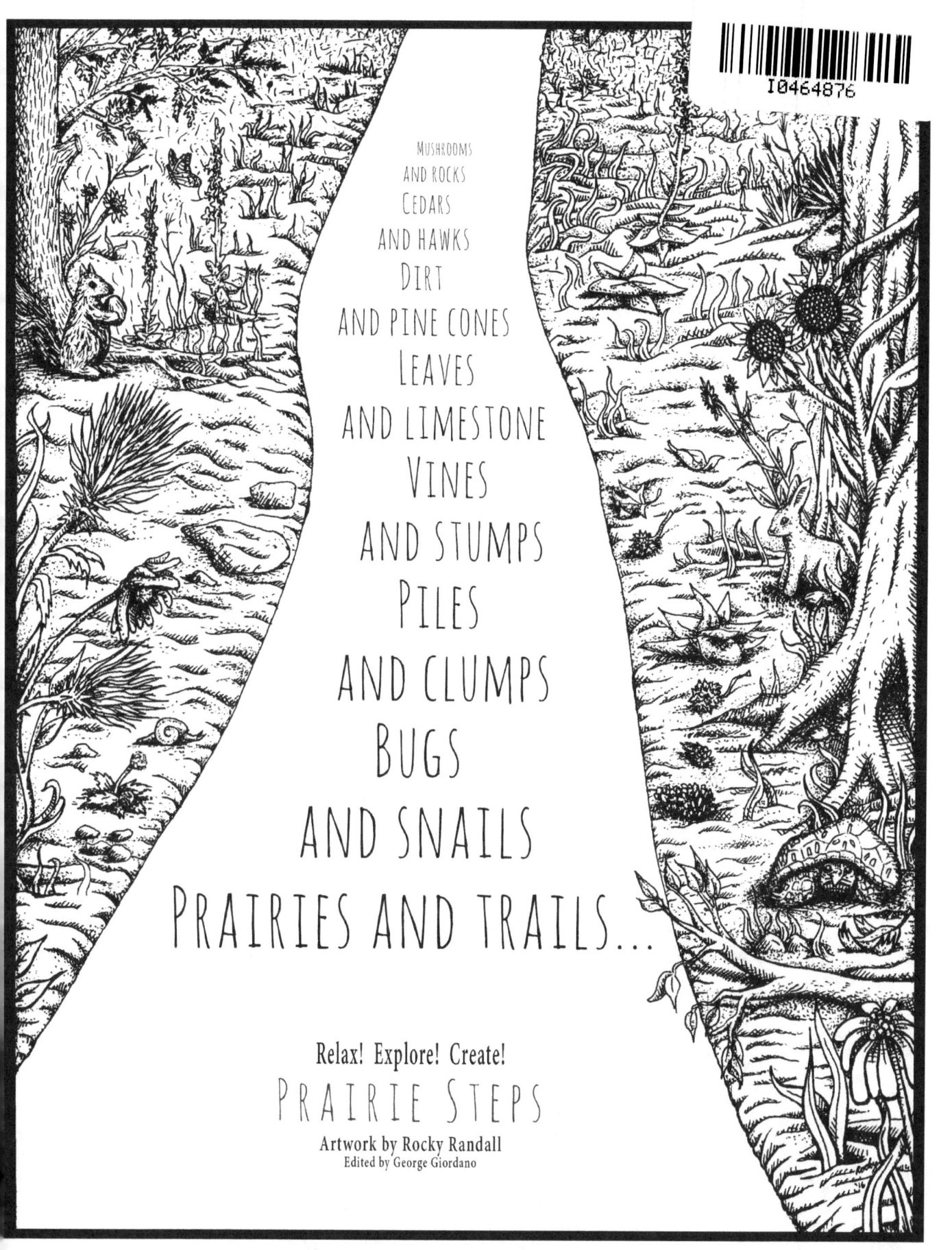

Mushrooms
and rocks
Cedars
and hawks
Dirt
and pine cones
Leaves
and limestone
Vines
and stumps
Piles
and clumps
Bugs
and snails
Prairies and trails...

Relax! Explore! Create!

PRAIRIE STEPS

Artwork by Rocky Randall
Edited by George Giordano

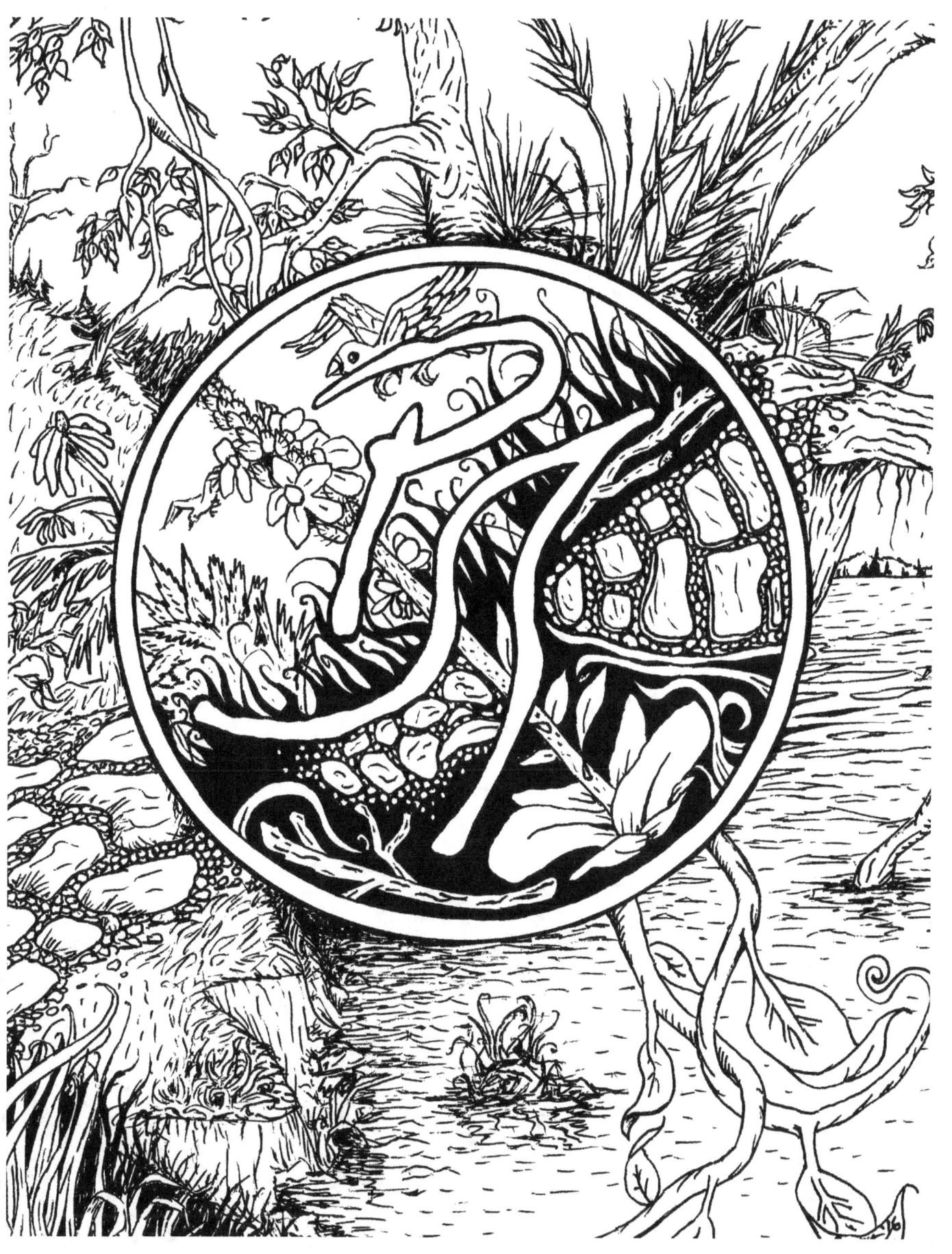

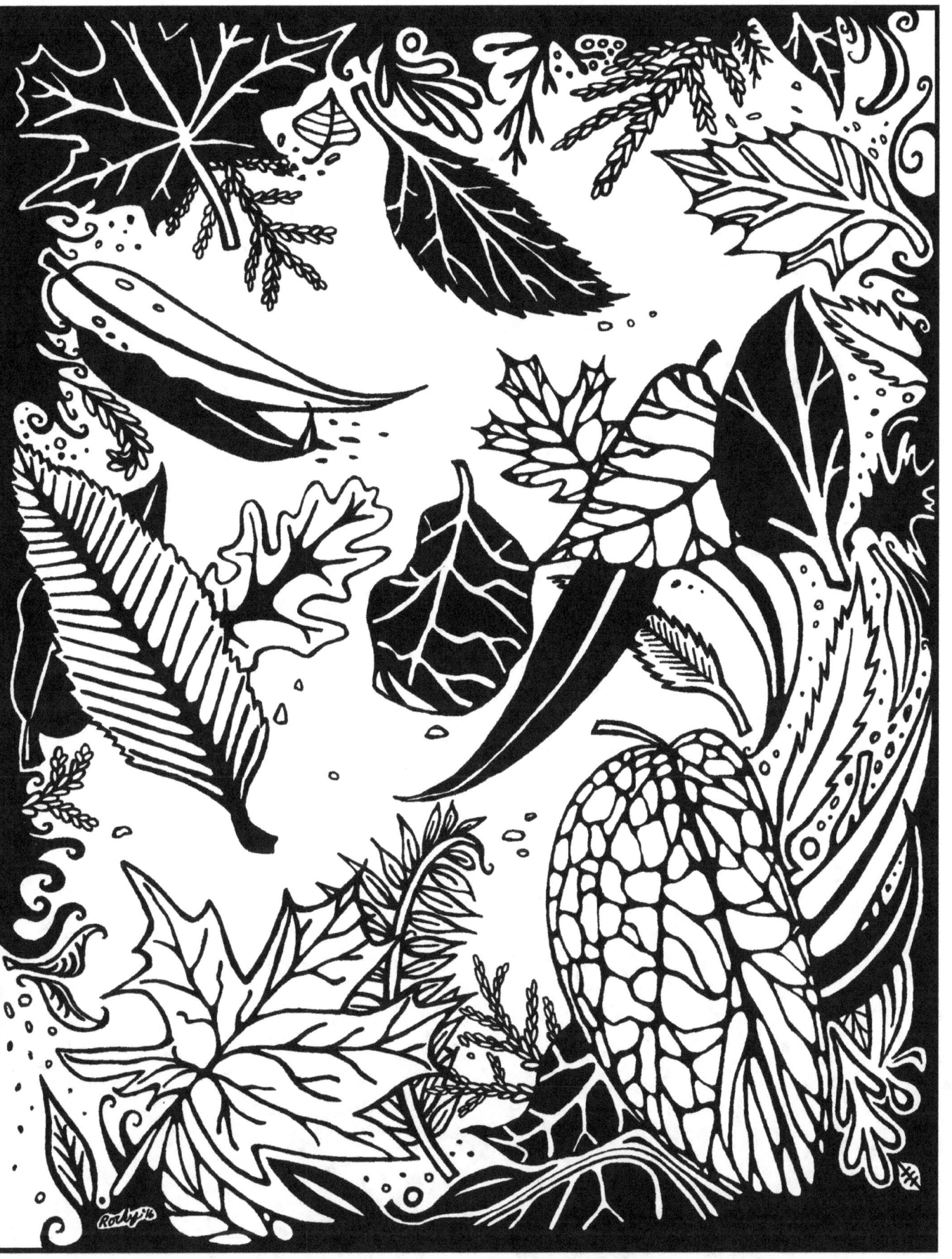

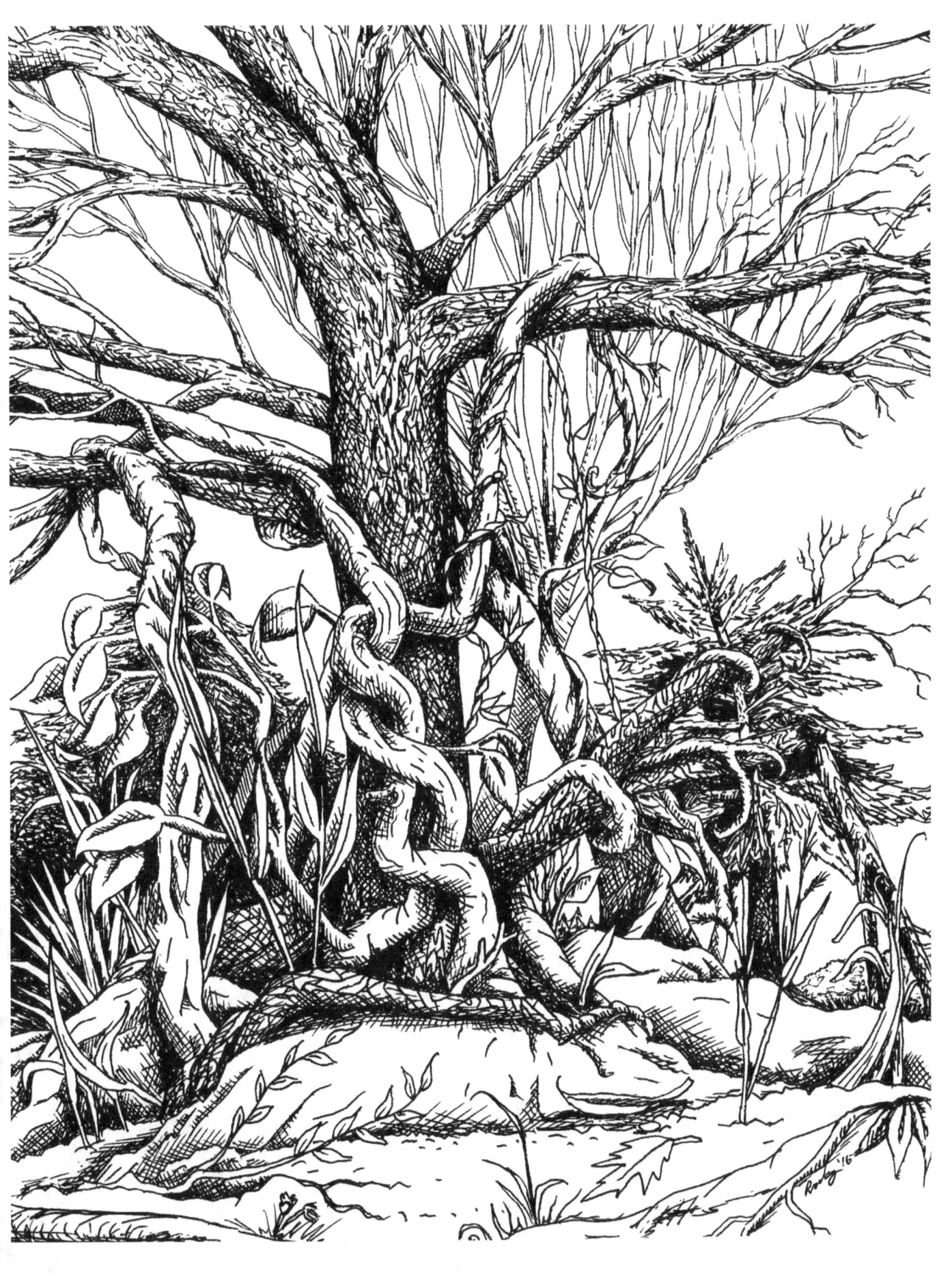

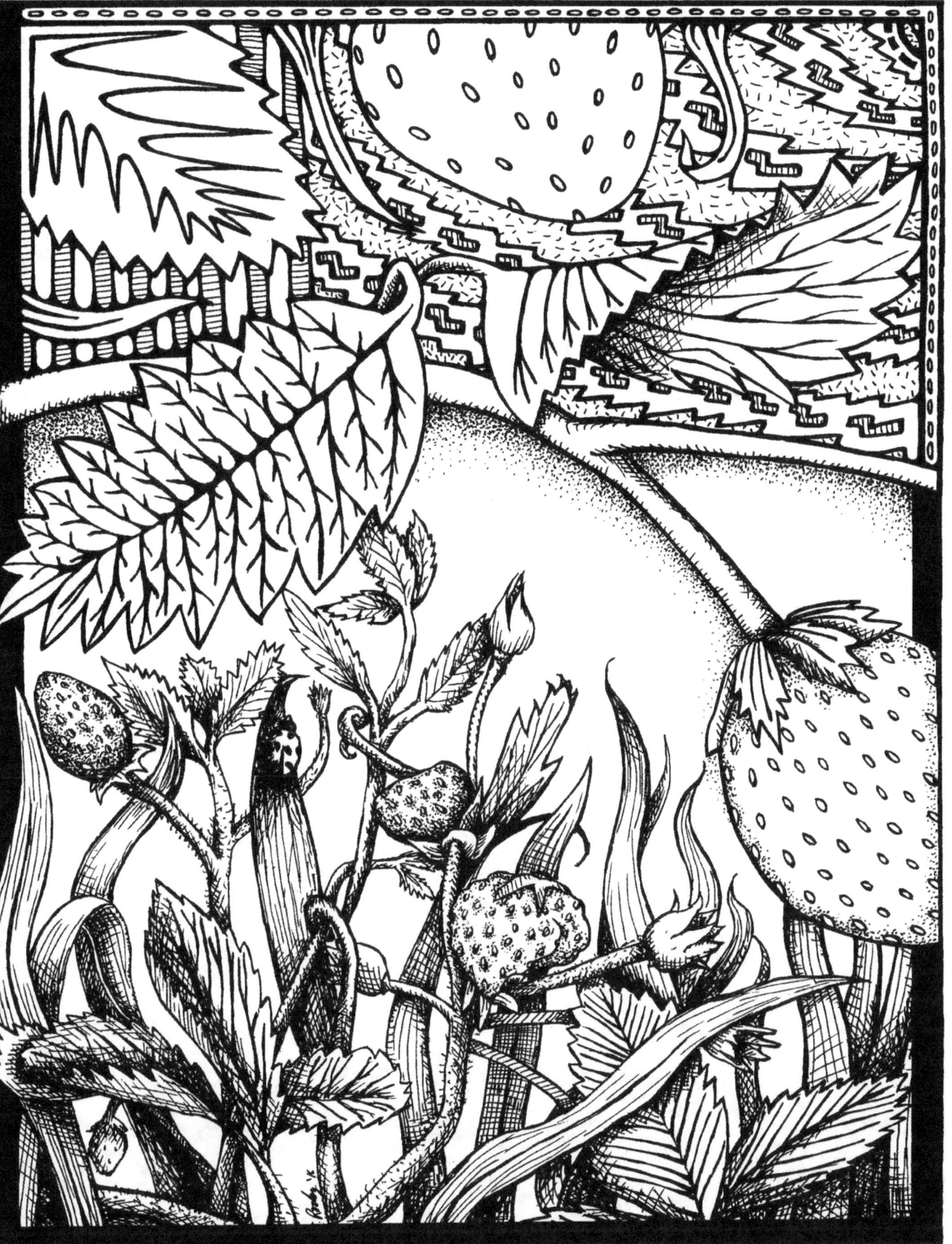

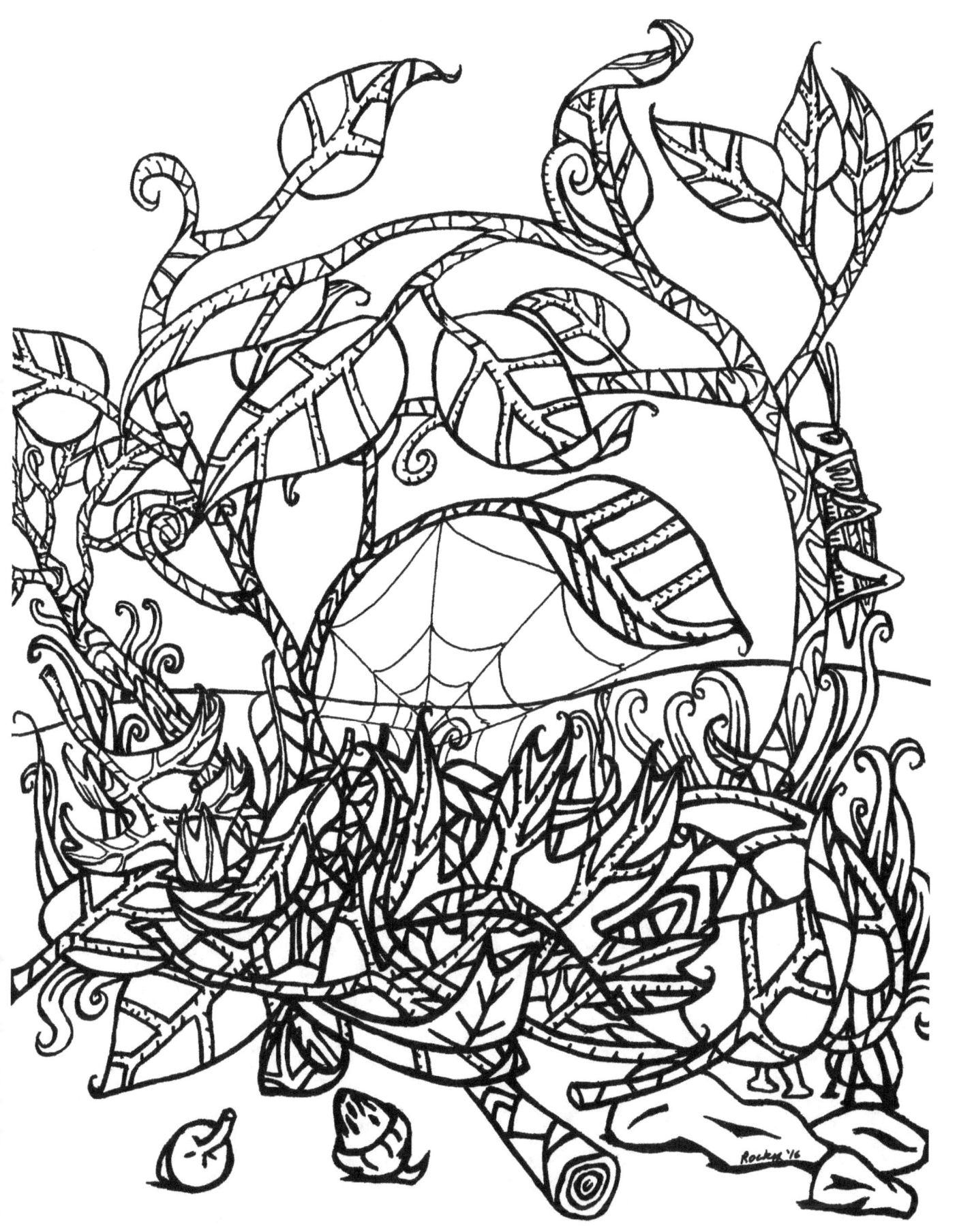

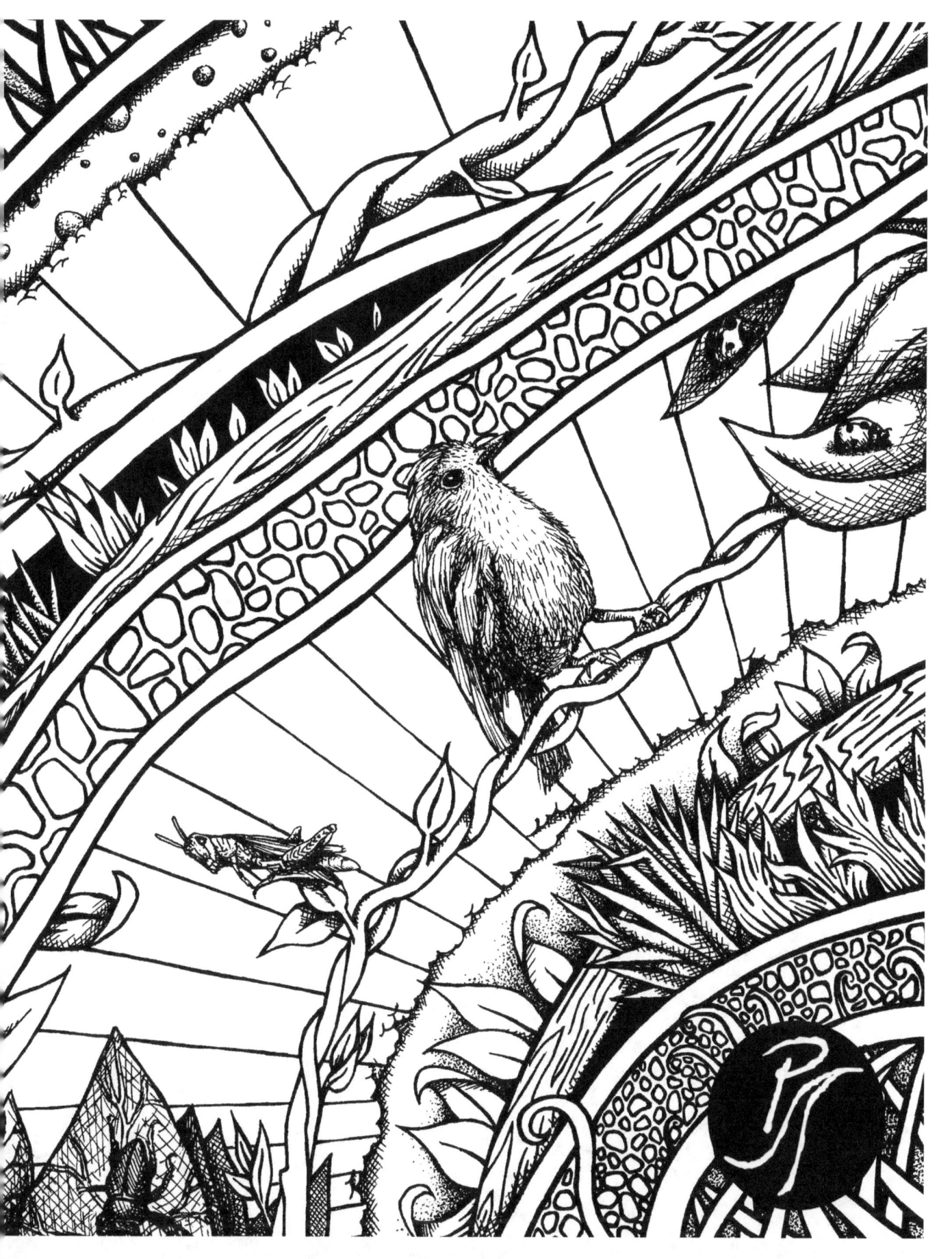

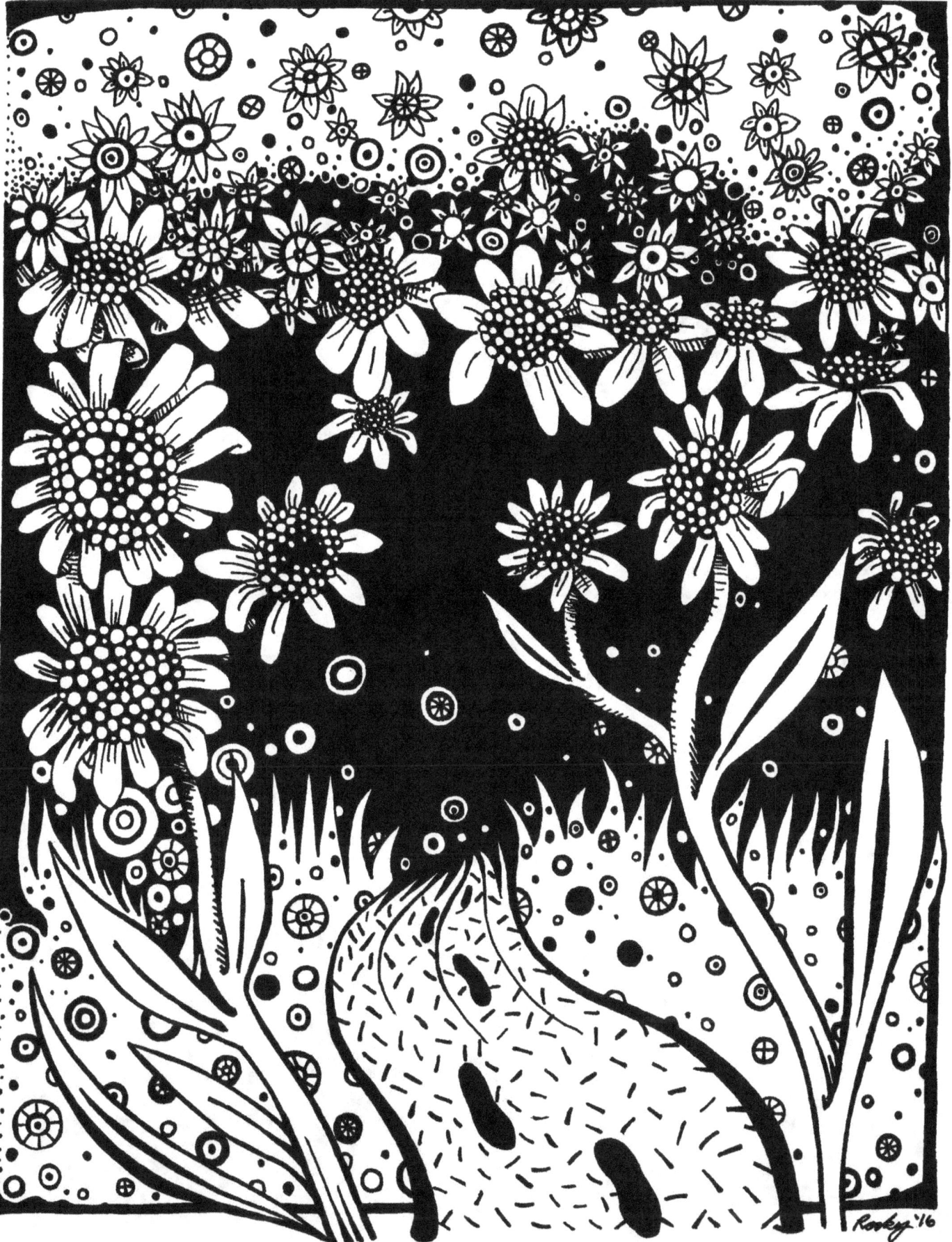

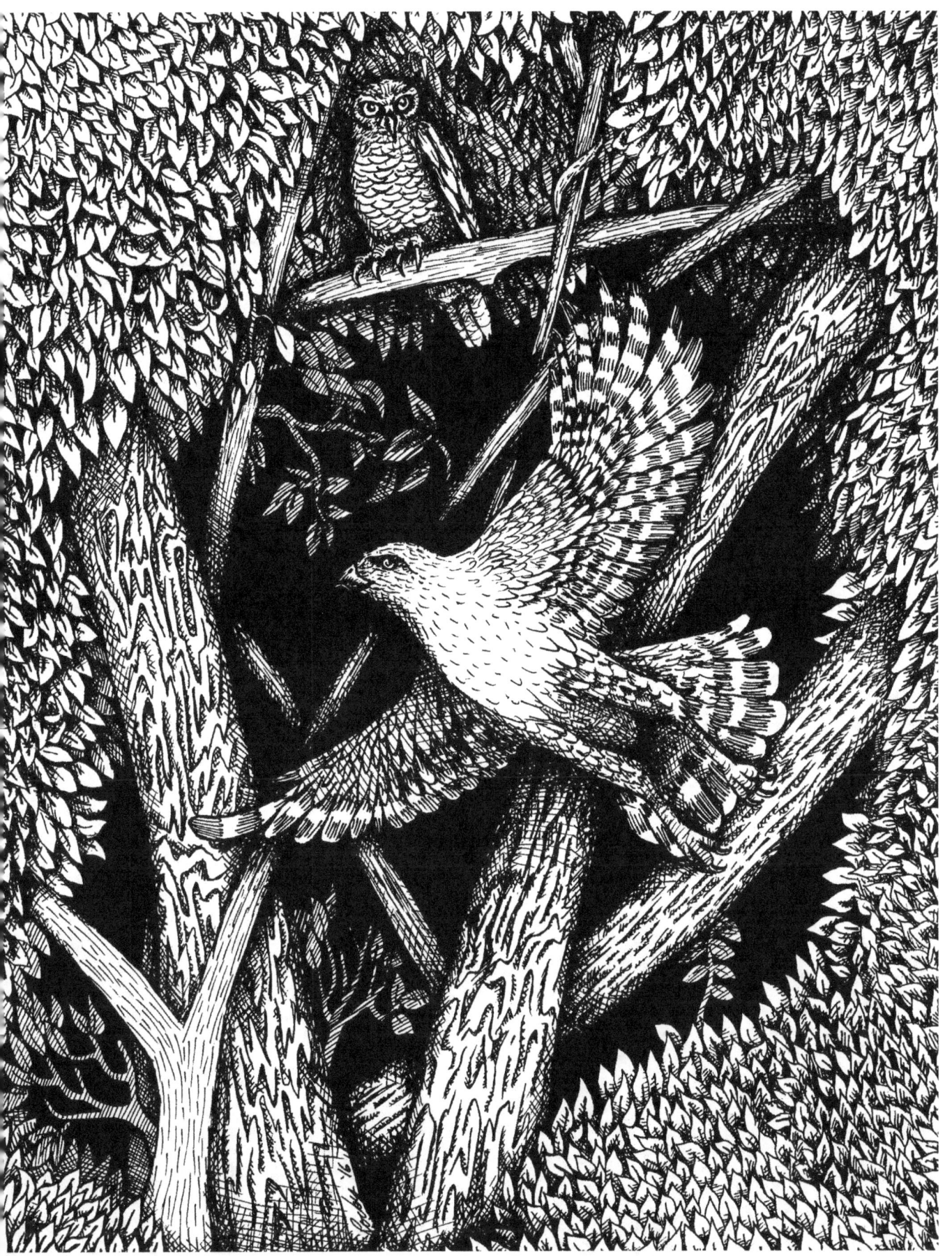

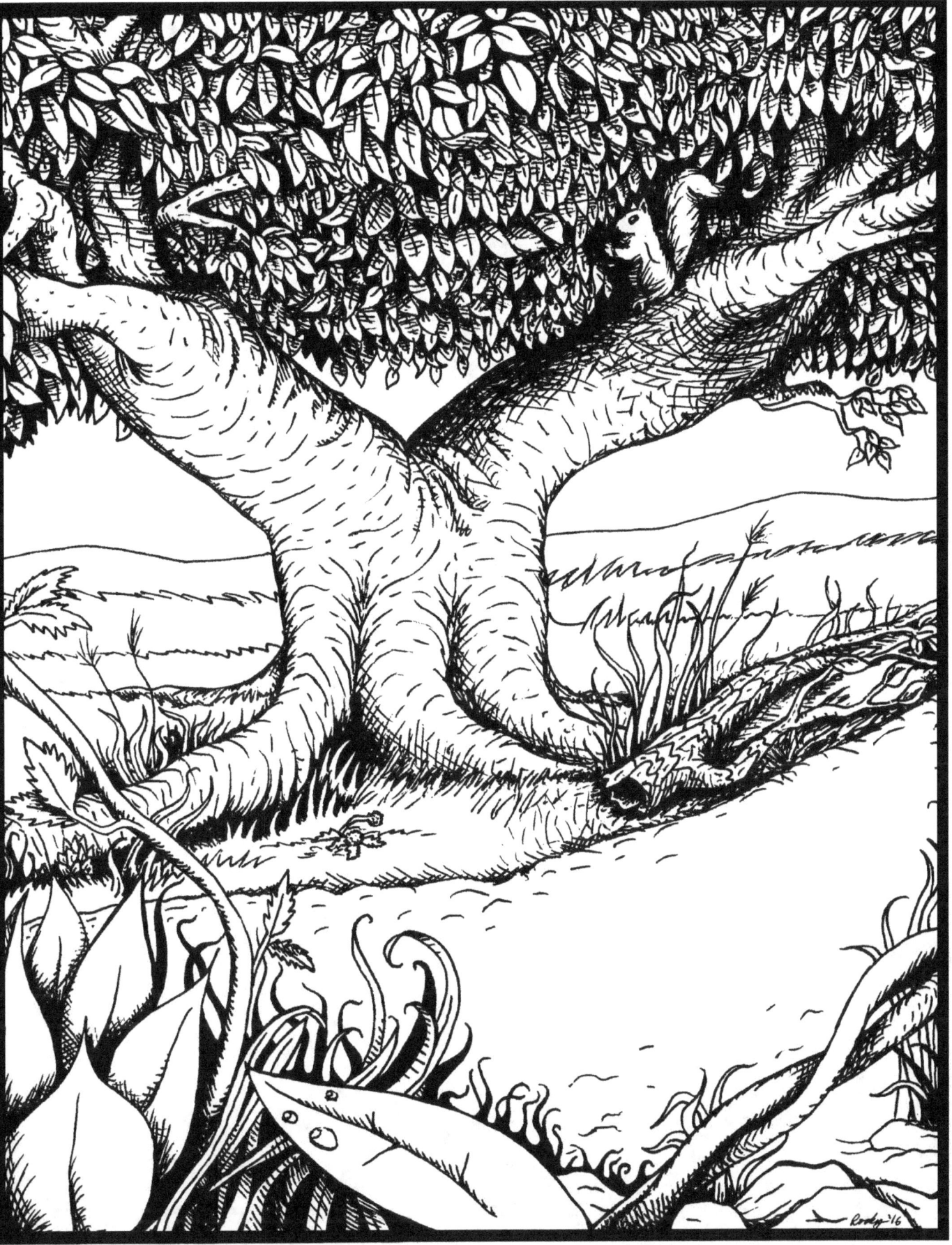

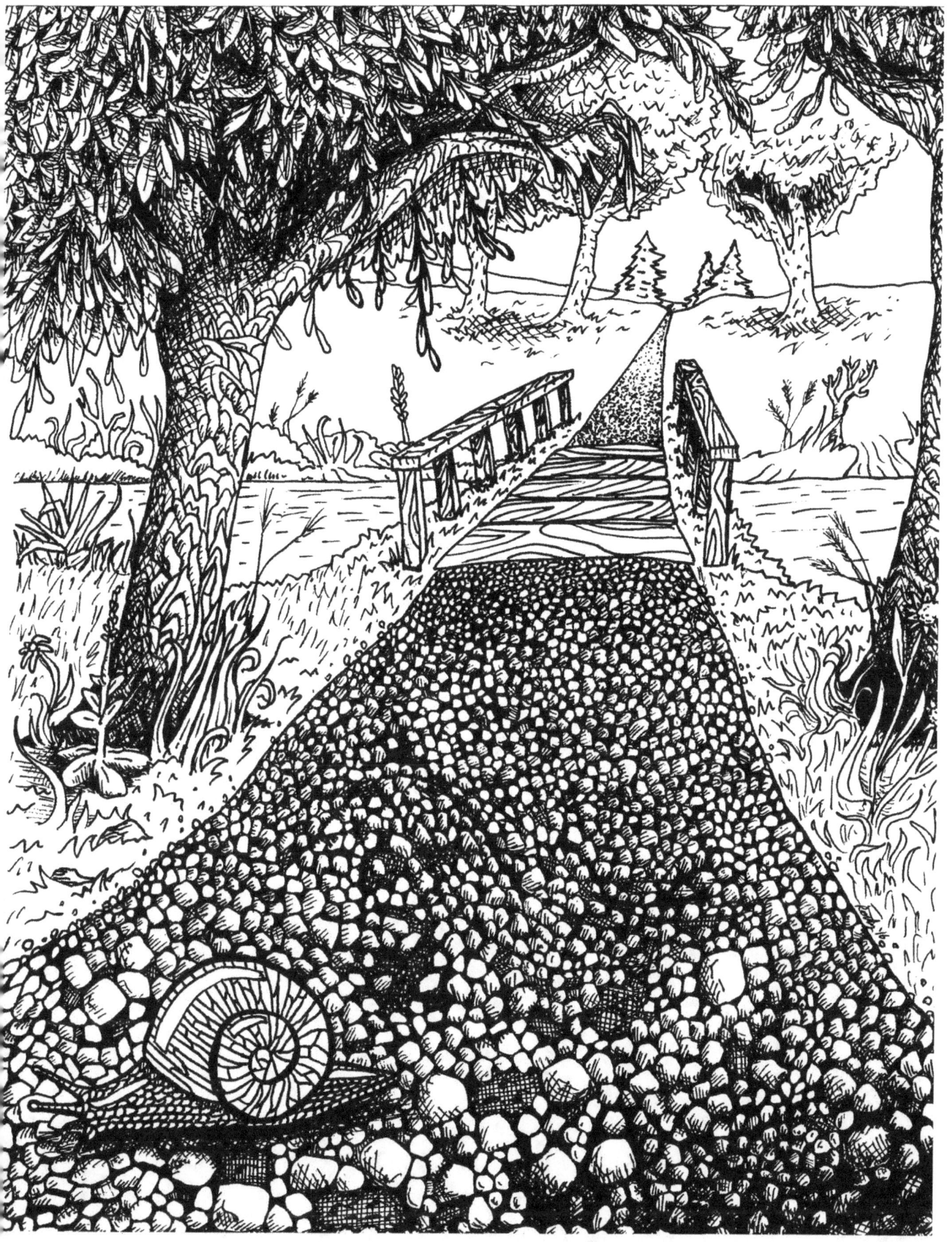

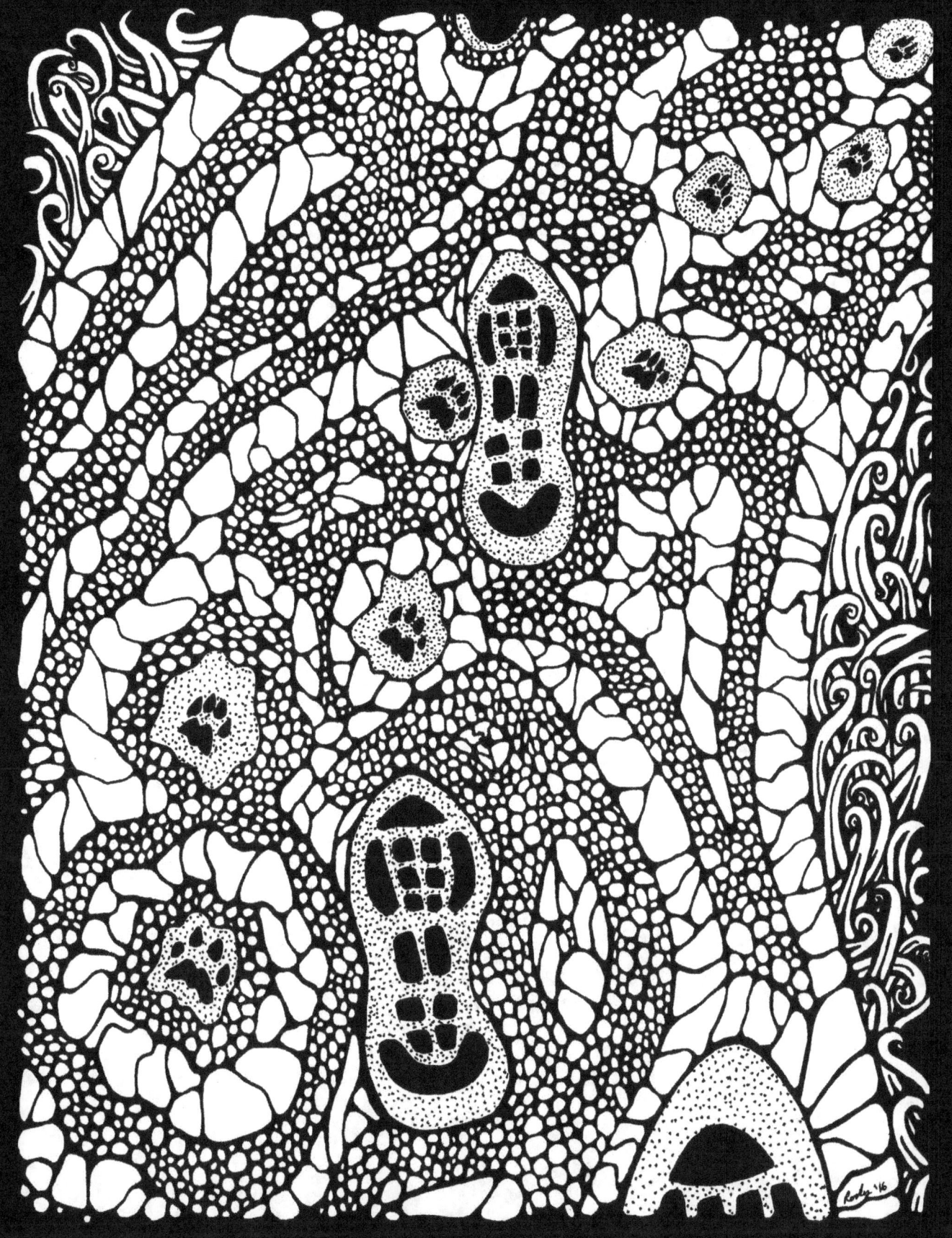

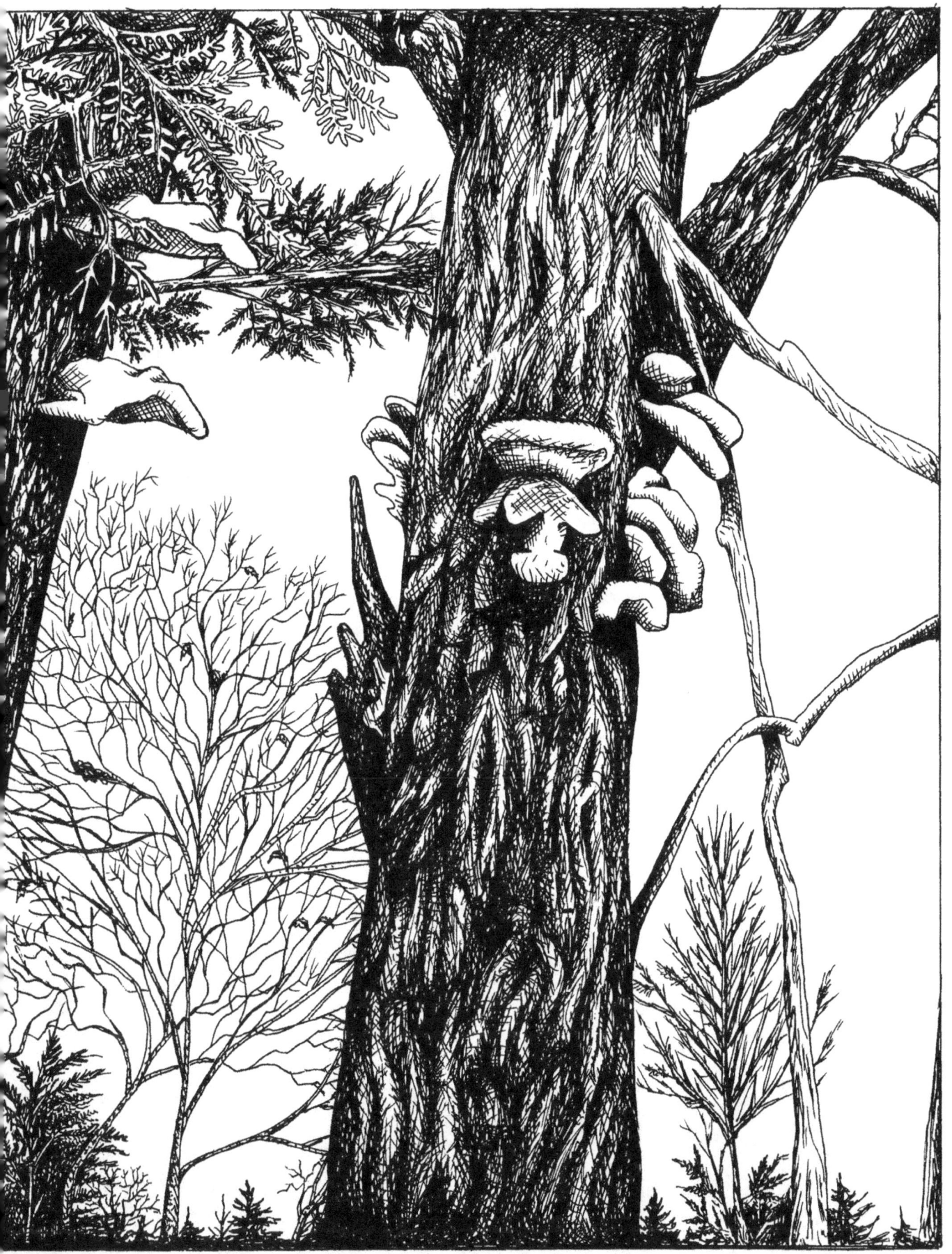

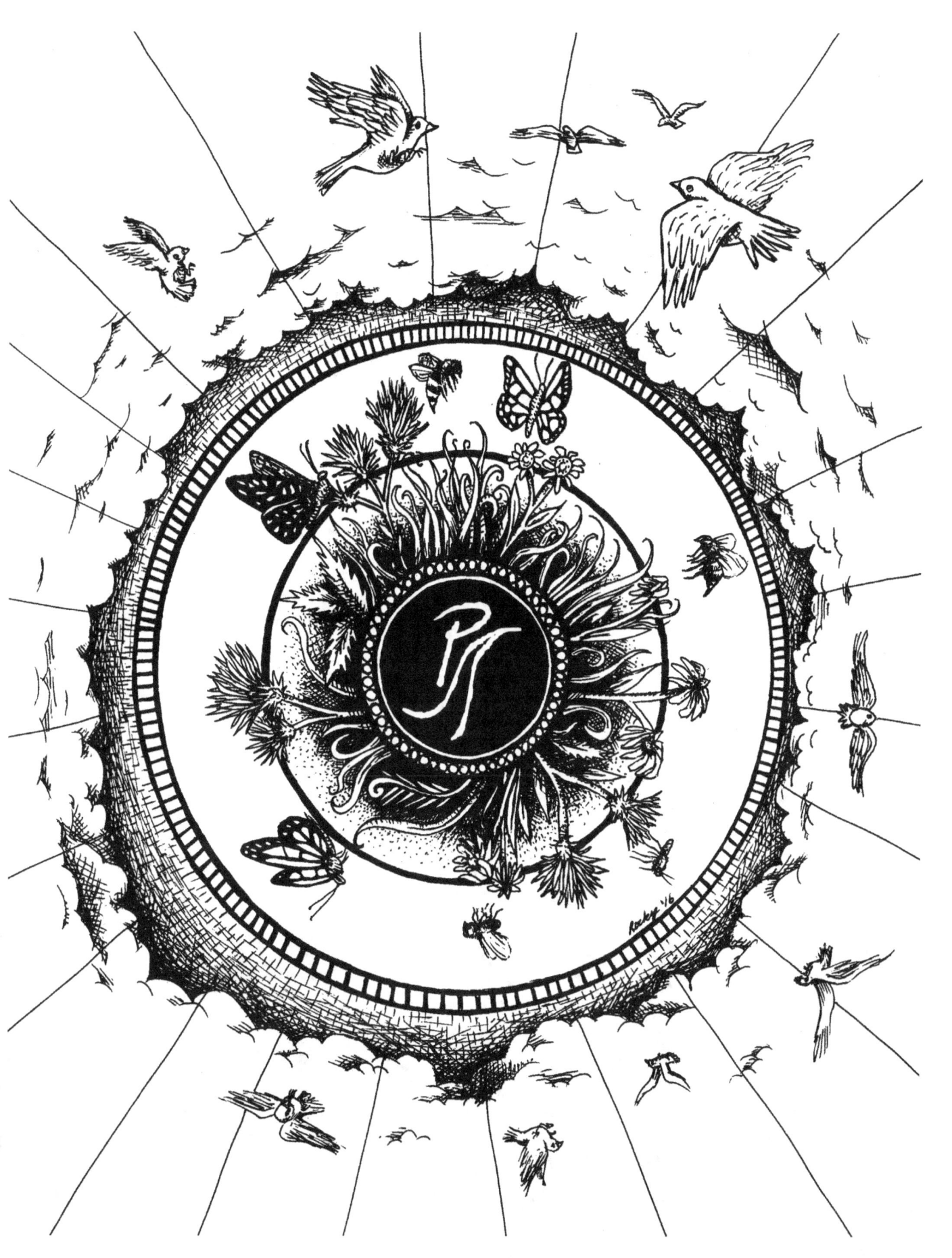

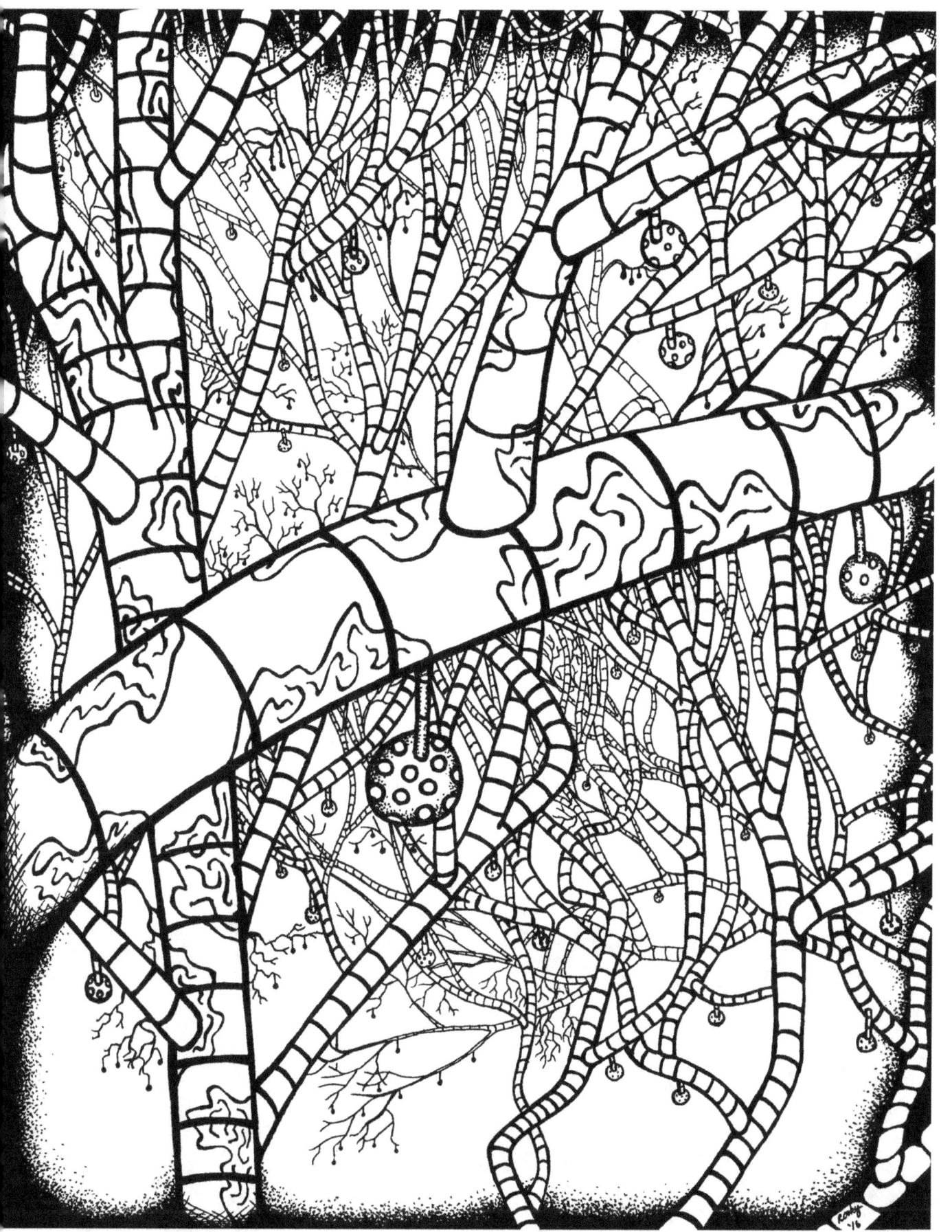

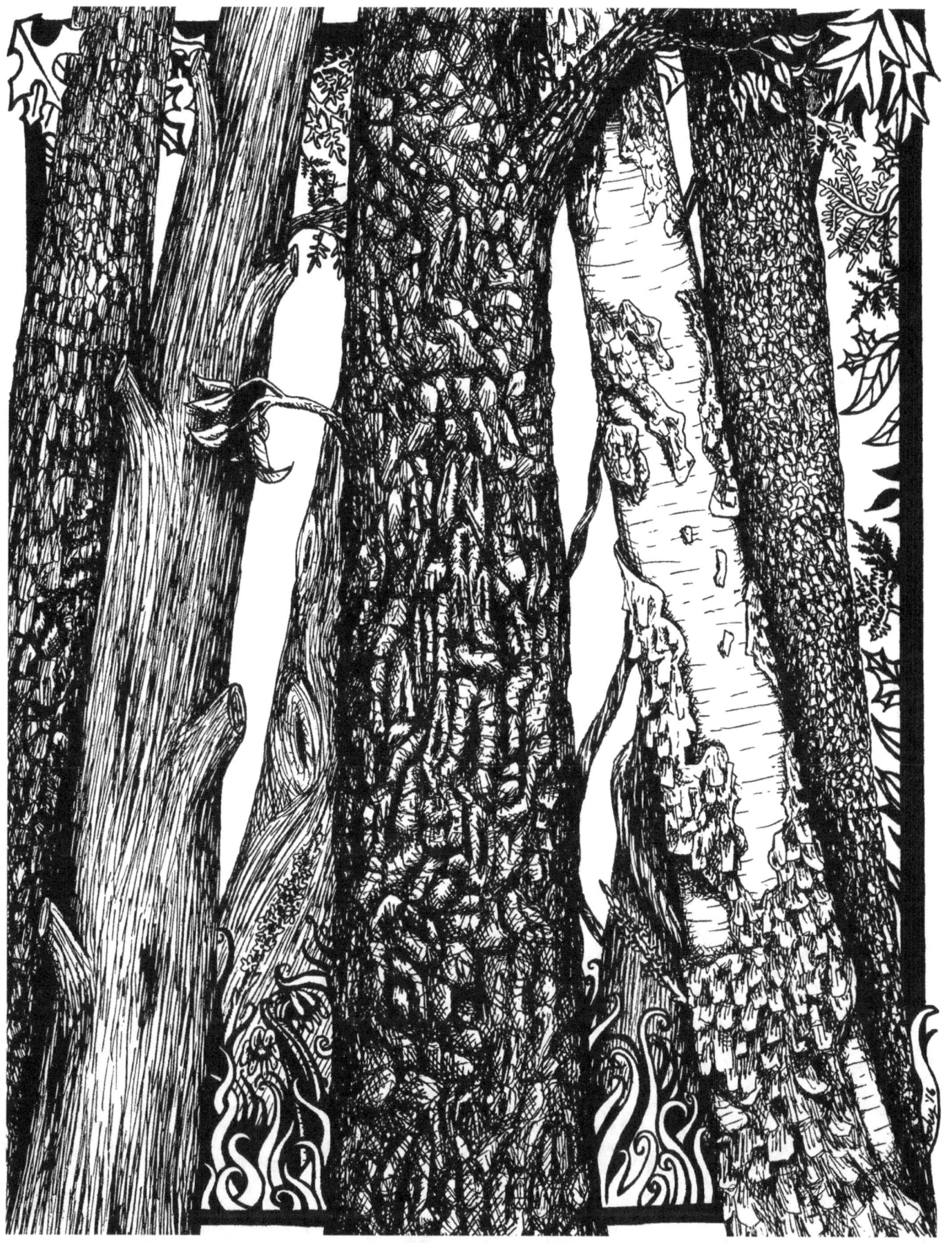

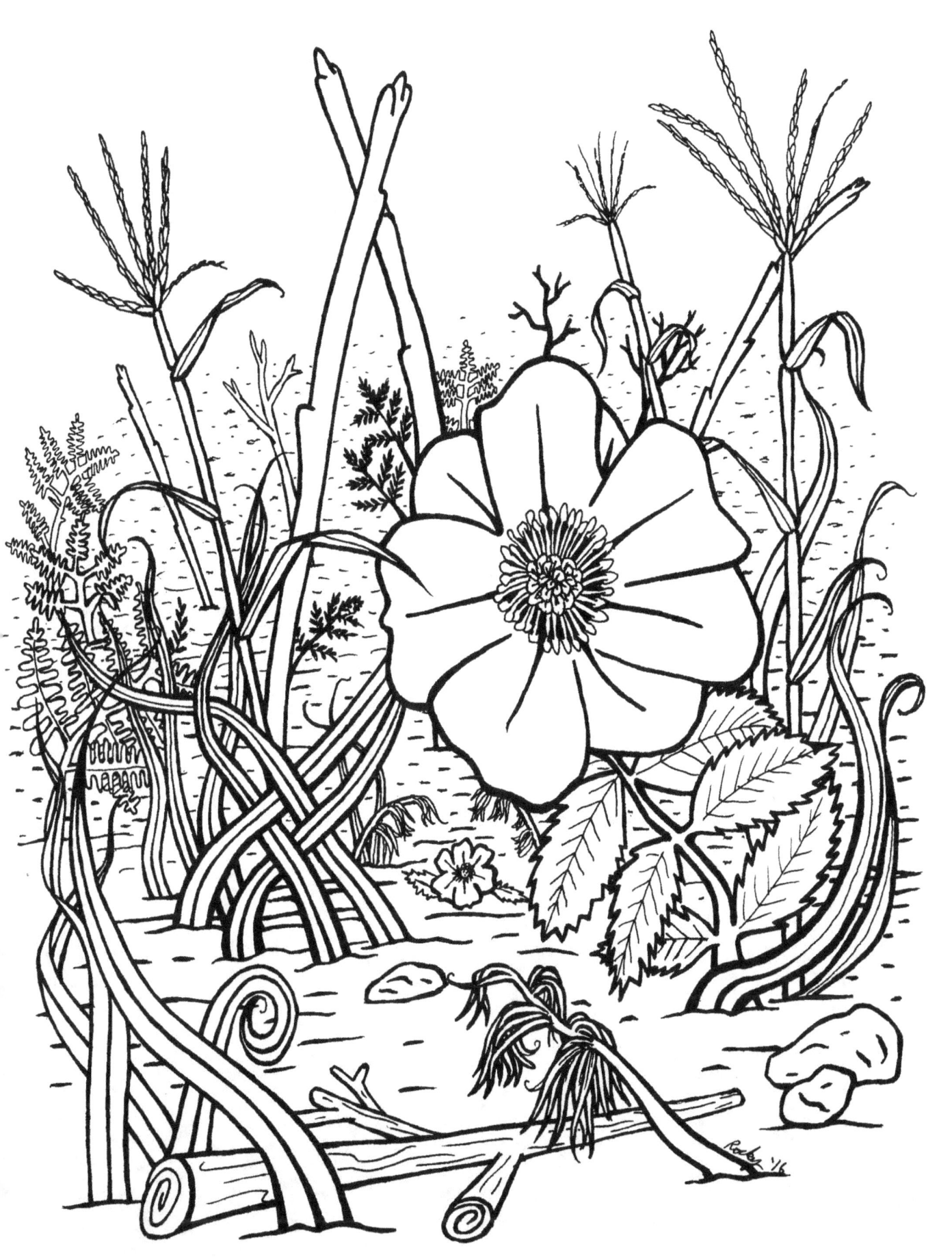

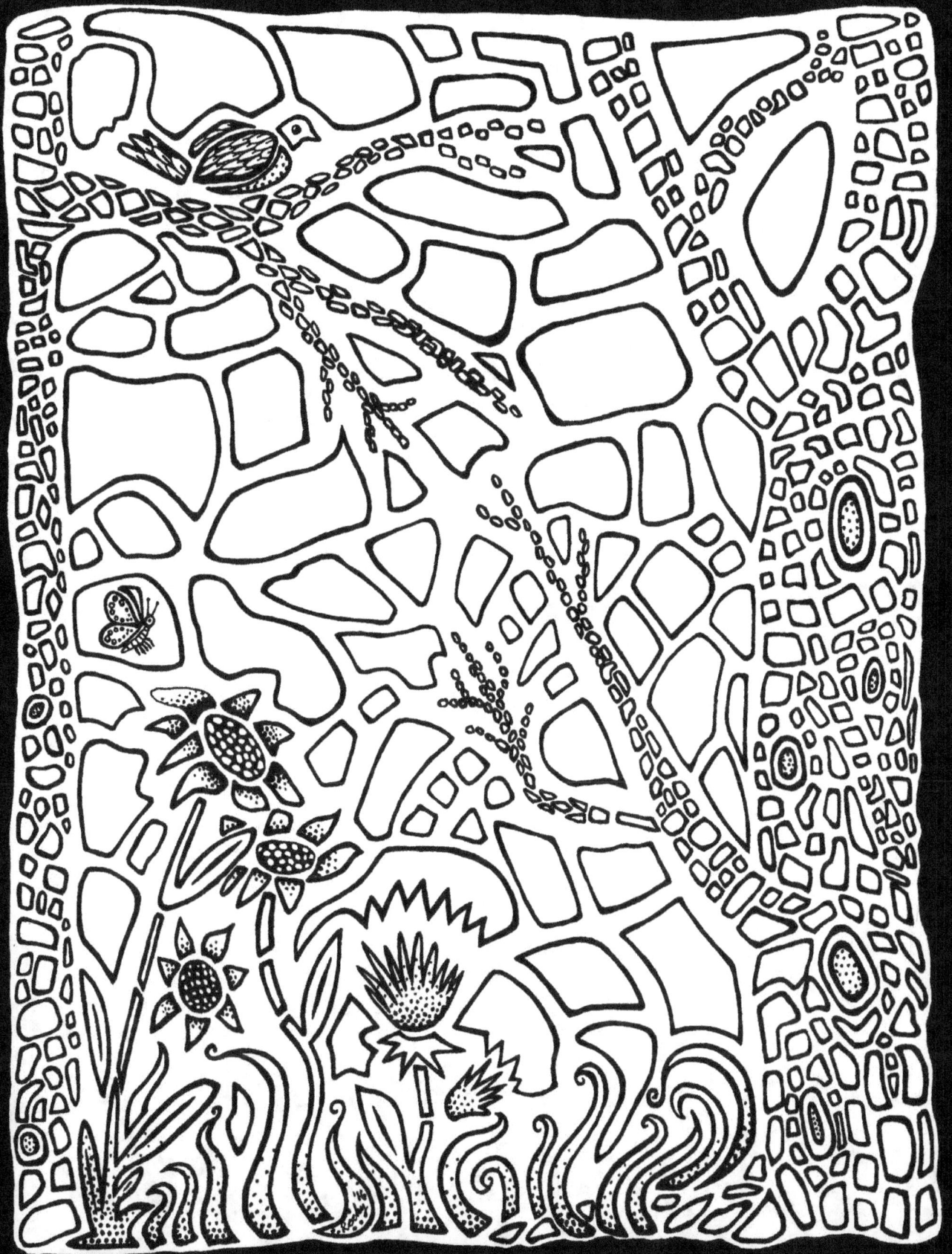

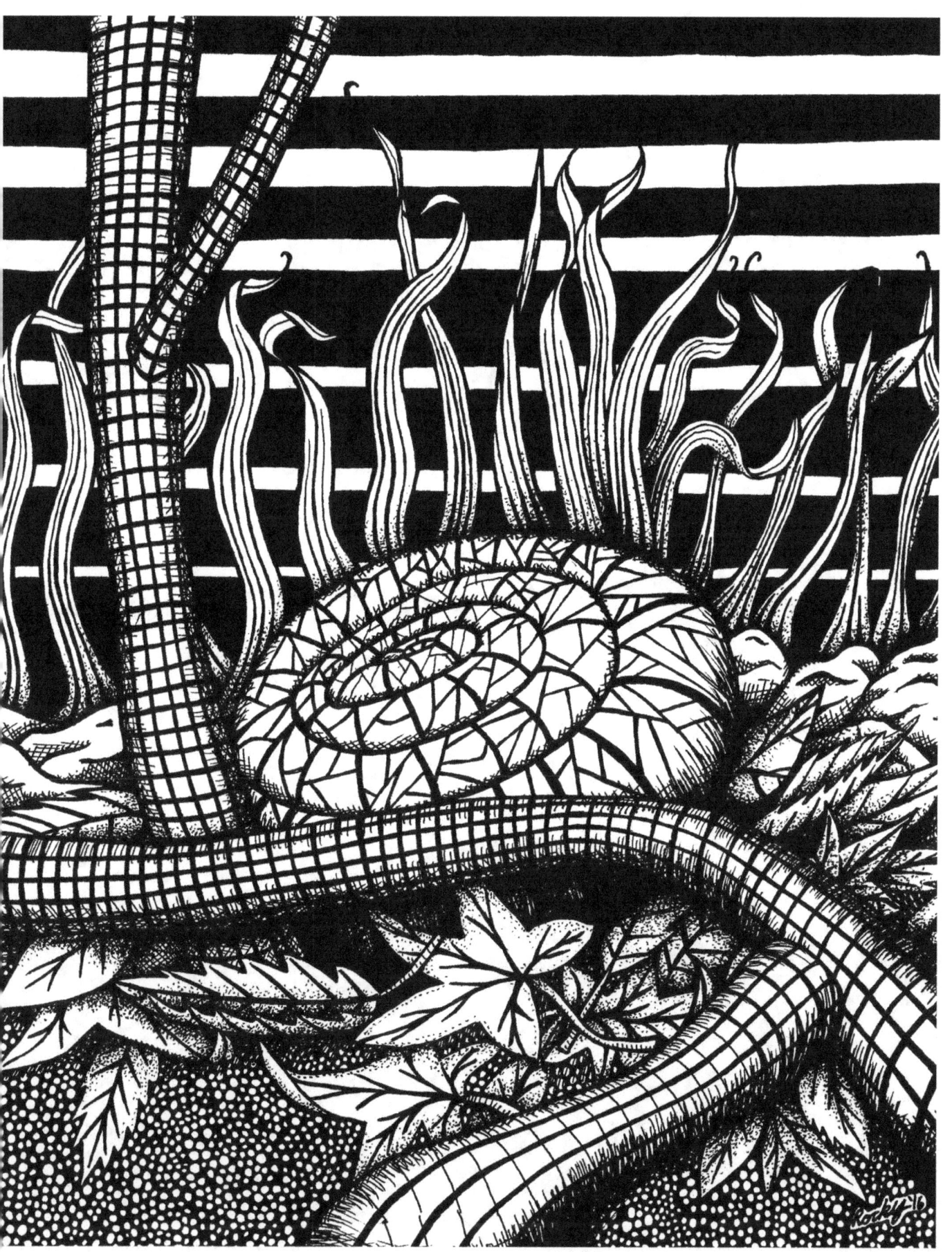

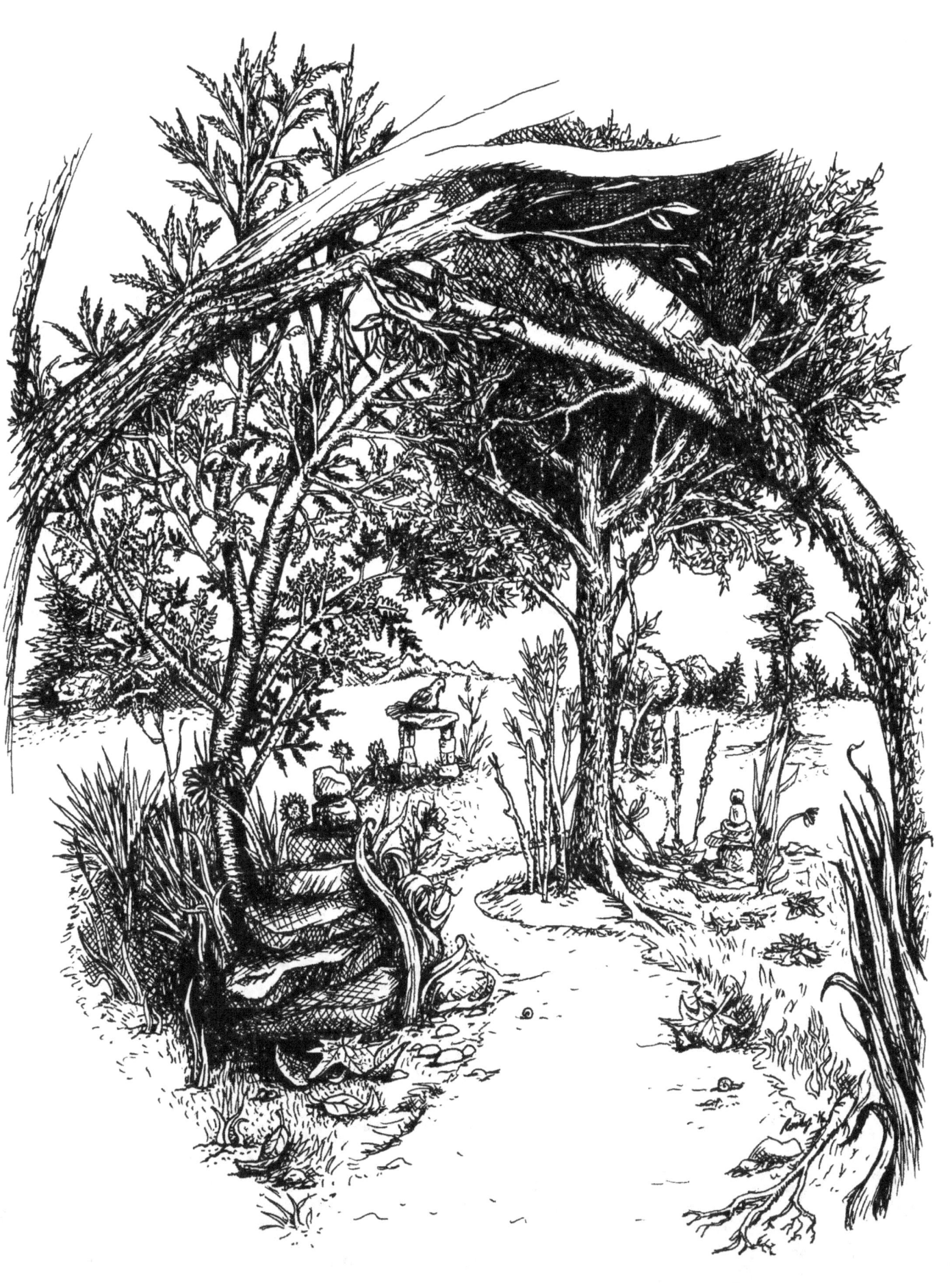

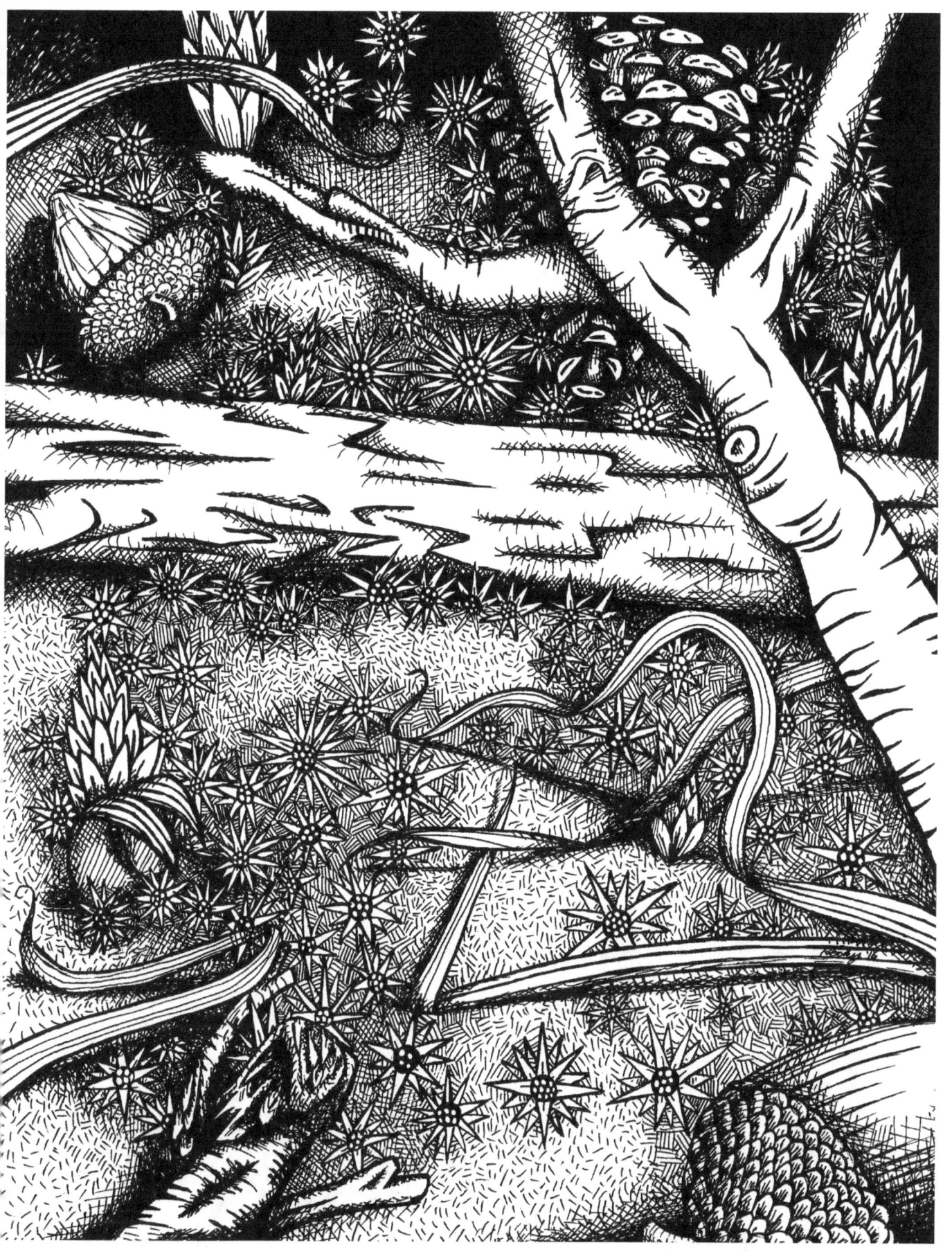

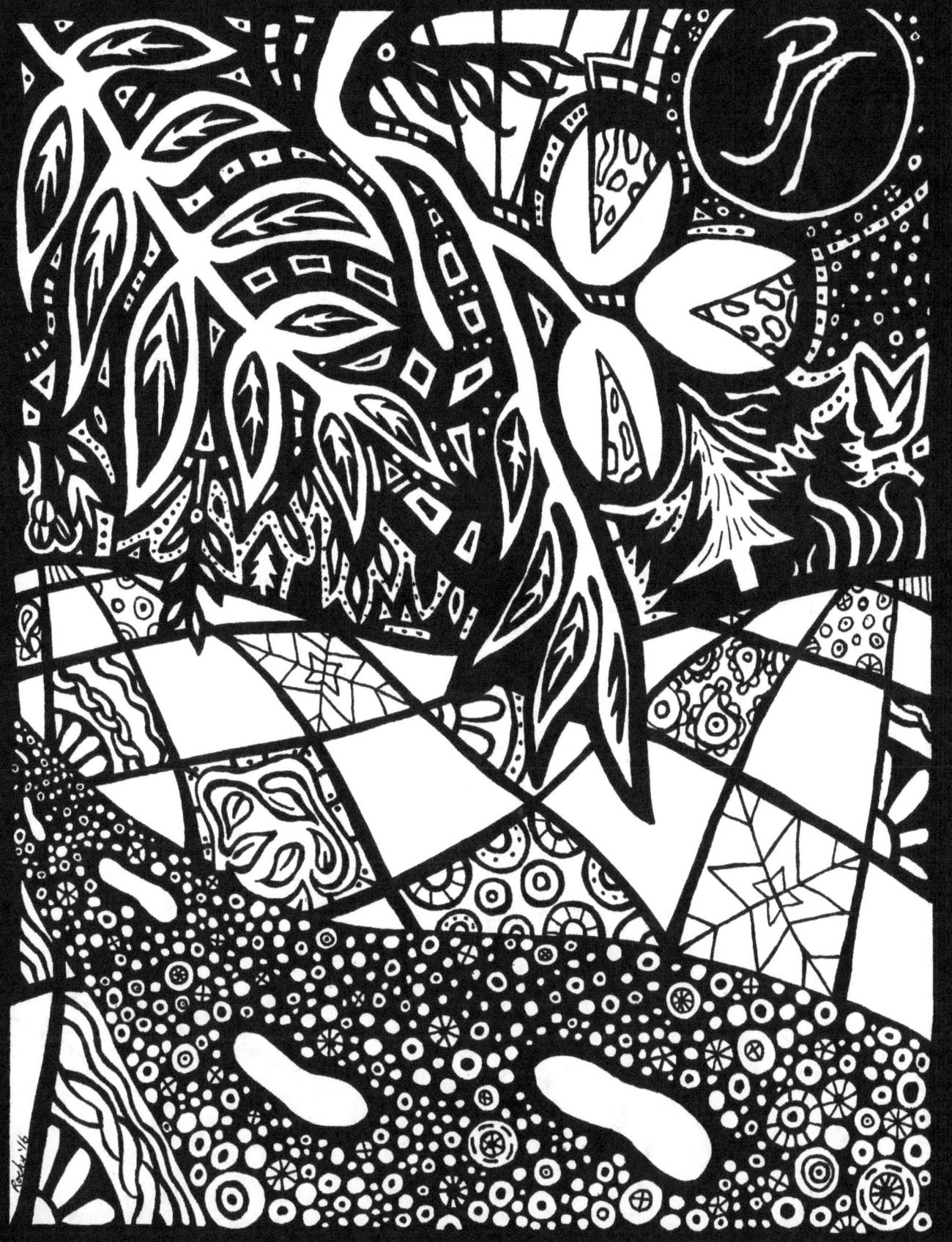

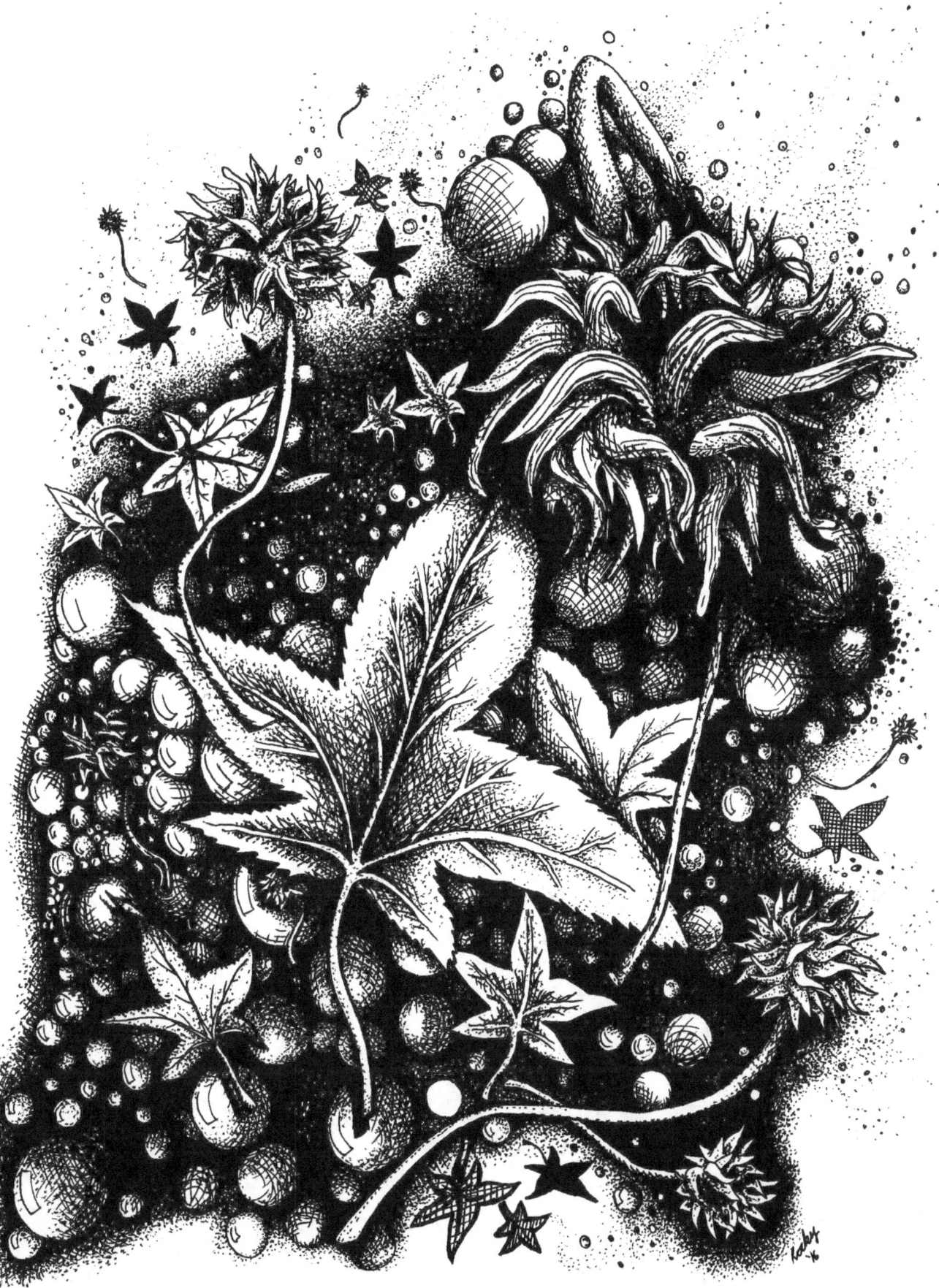

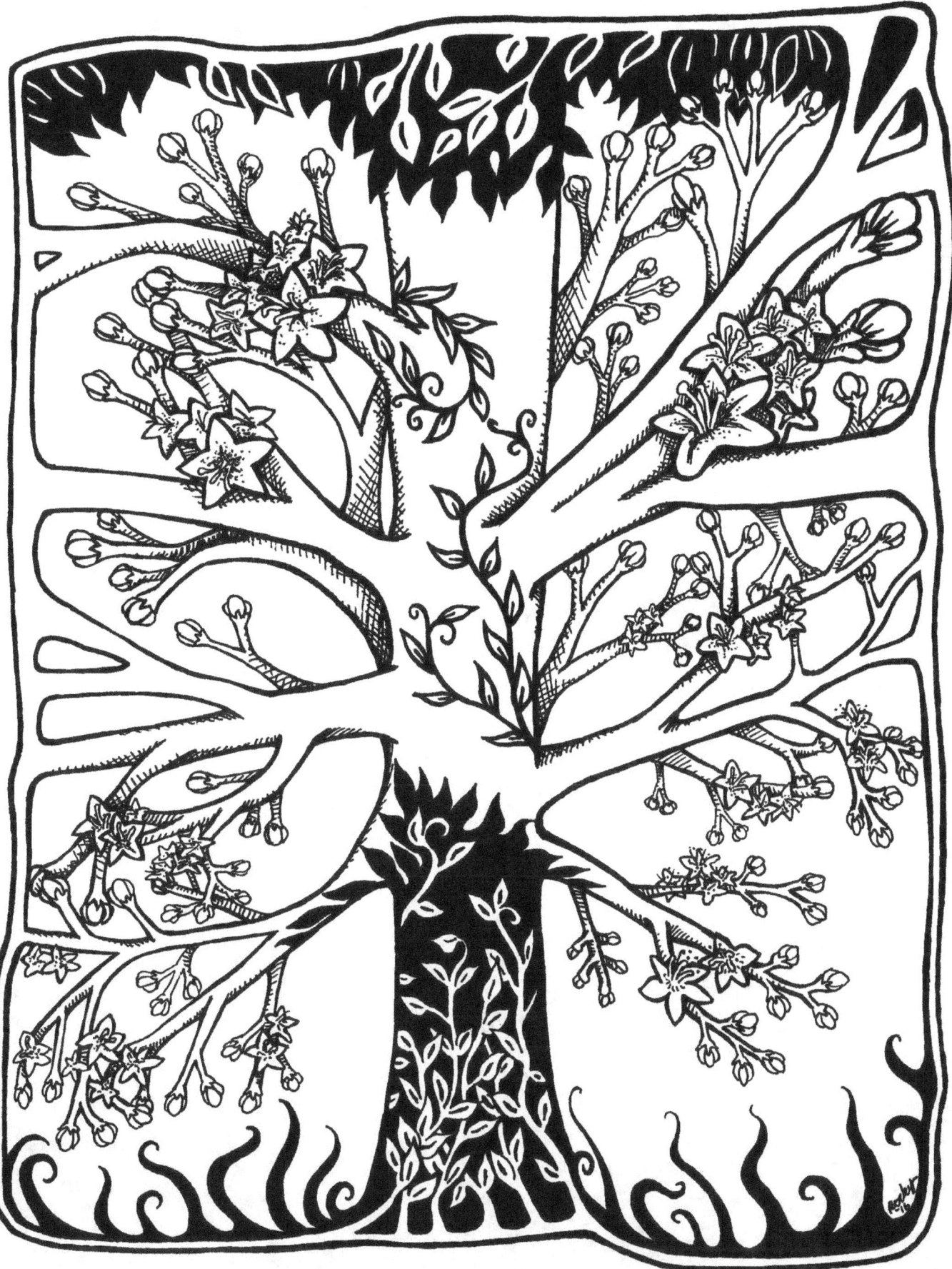

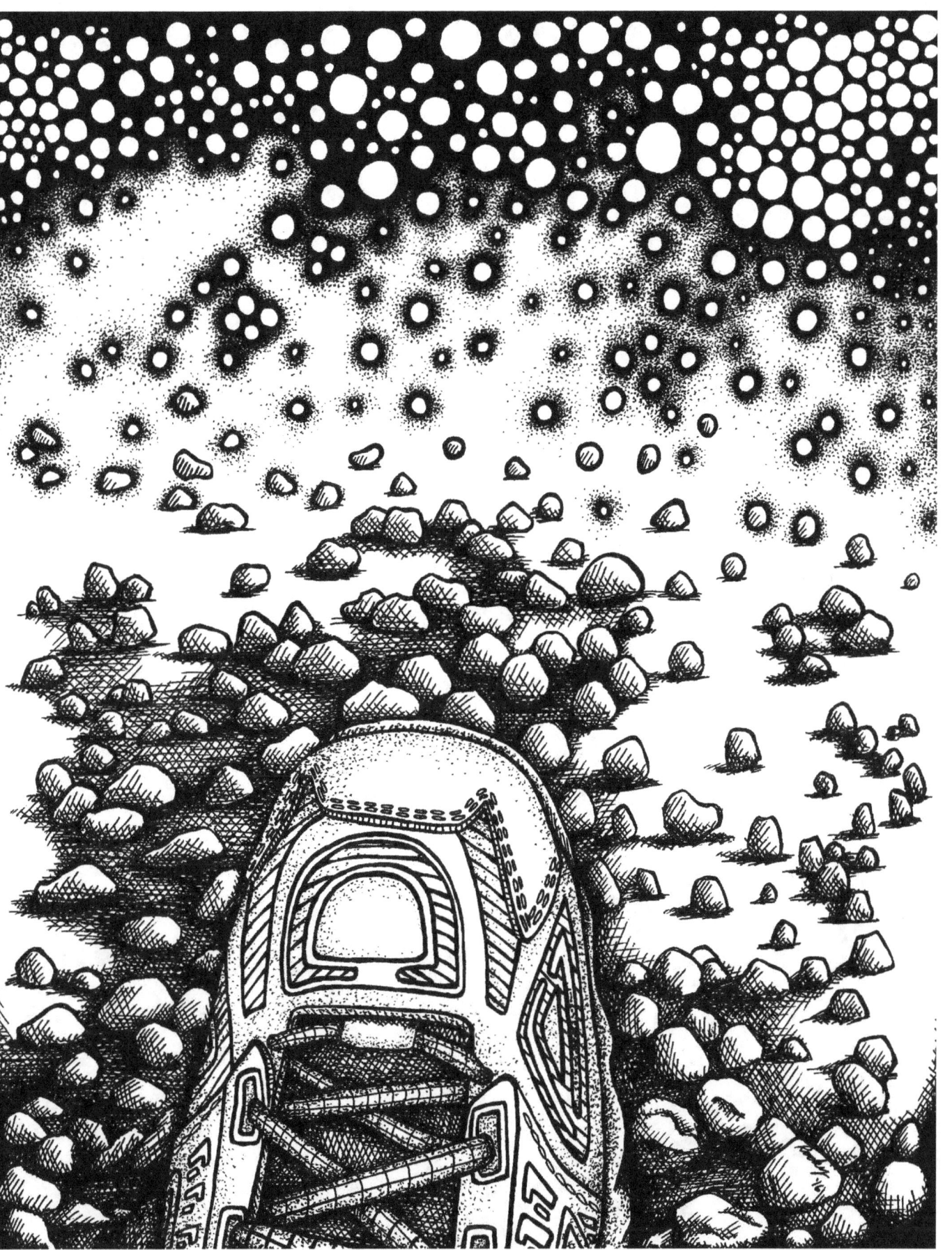

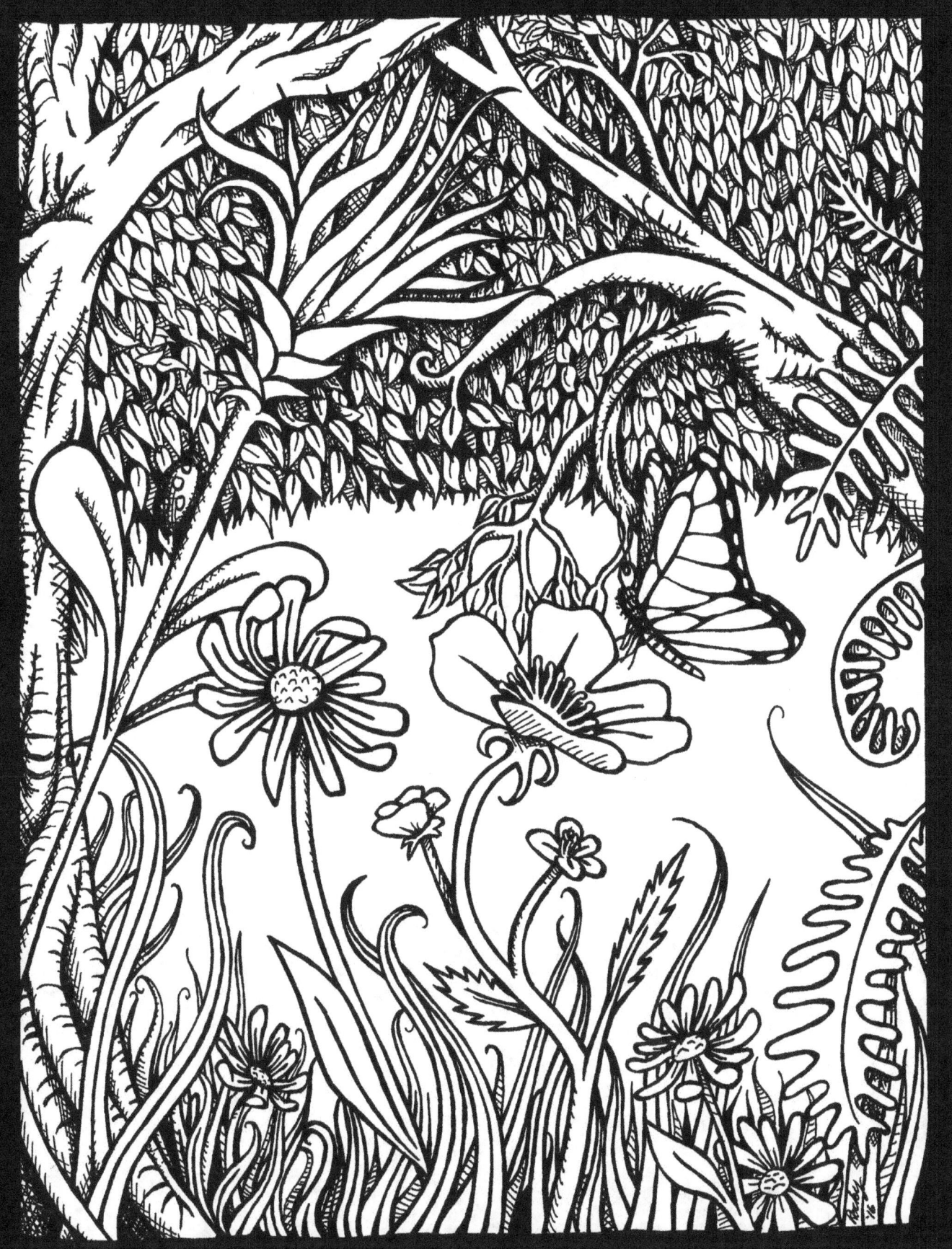

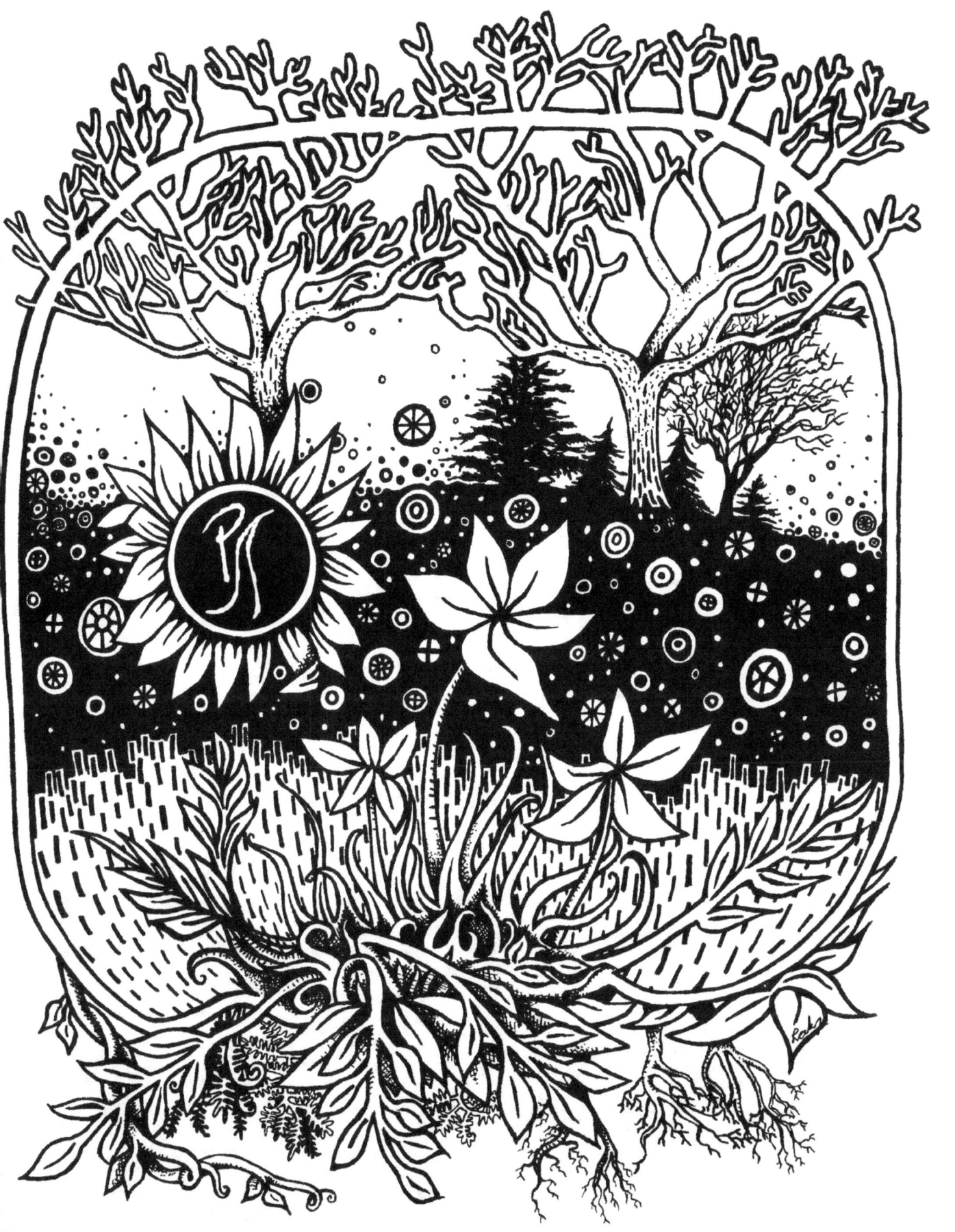

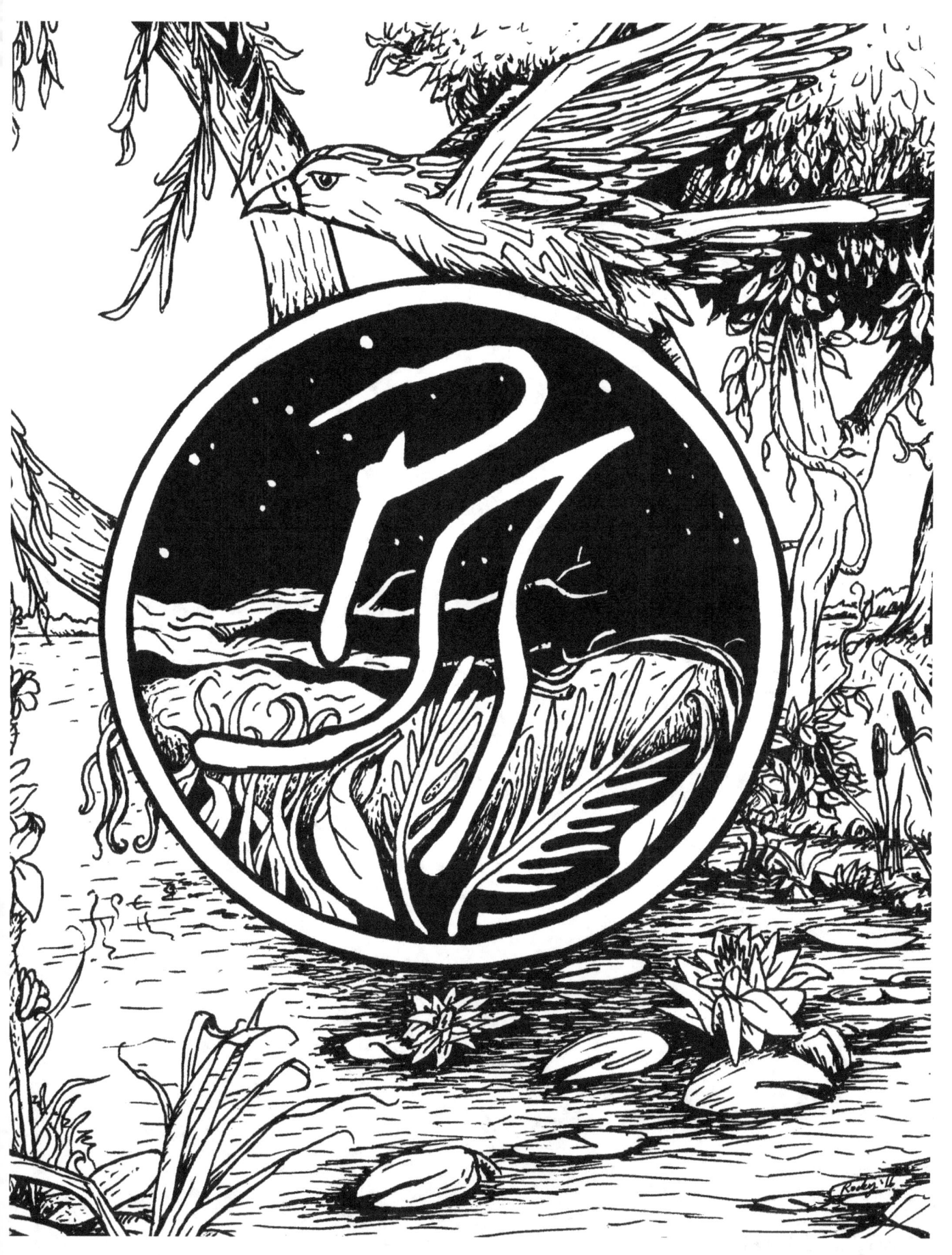